EMILY BEAR

DIVERSITY

Jordan King Music USA

P.O. Box 271, Rockford, IL 61105

ISBN: 978-0-9826015-4-9

TABLE OF CONTENTS

ZUILL BAILEY

FRANCISCO MELA &
CARLITOS DEL PUERTO

QUINCY JONES

Emily Bear is an eleven year old pianist and composer who has been making music her whole life. She started composing at age 3, began piano lessons at age 4, and won the ASCAP Morton Gould Young Composer of the Year Award at the age of 6. Since then, she has composed countless pieces for piano and other instruments, composed and orchestrated symphonies, scored films, performed classical repertoire, and honed her deep connection to Jazz.

Quincy Jones has been both a mentor and guide to Emily, culminating in this CD which he produced, featuring 13 of Emily's original pieces performed by jazz trio — with special guest Zuill Bailey.

The title 'Diversity' represents the diversity of Emily's style as well as the diversity of the cultures that are her musical influences. In turn, through her music, Emily has touched the souls of countless people worldwide.

The songs on this CD were composed by Emily between the ages of 6 and 10. Whether it is a favorite cousin, a trip to the Italian countryside, or her beloved Q that inspired the songs on this CD, Emily takes us on a musical journey through an oasis of sound.

Northern Lights

MUSIC BY
EMILY BEAR

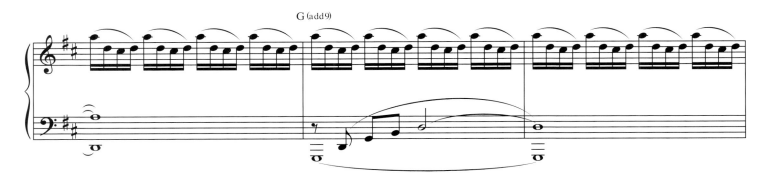

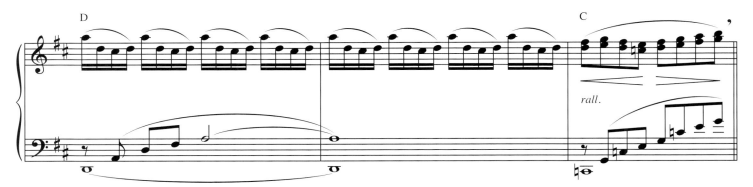

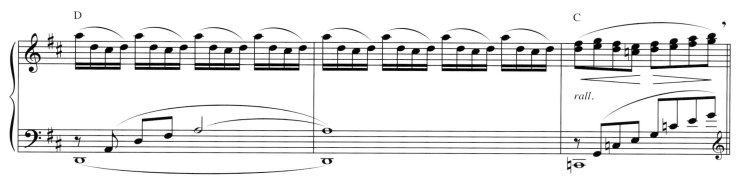

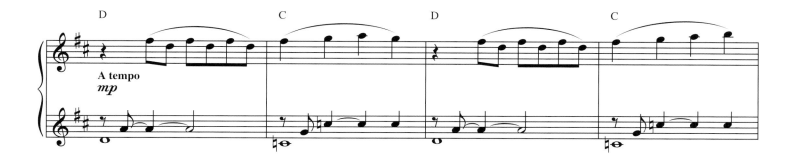

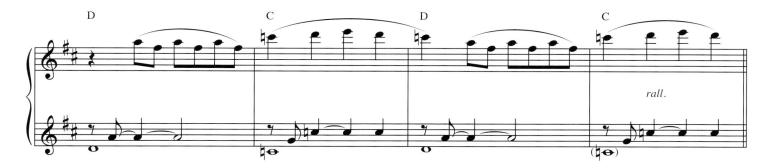

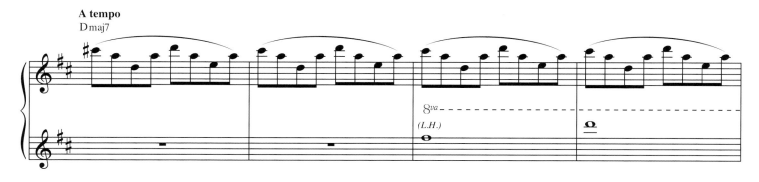

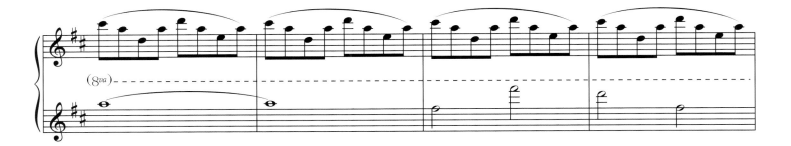

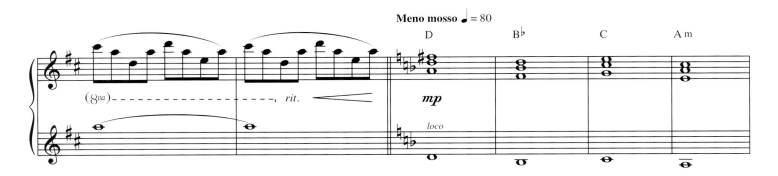

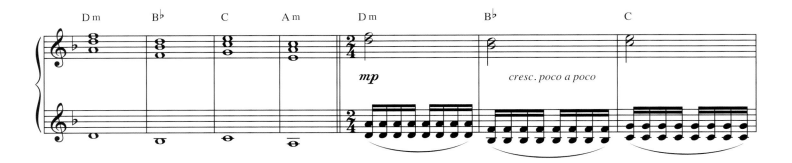

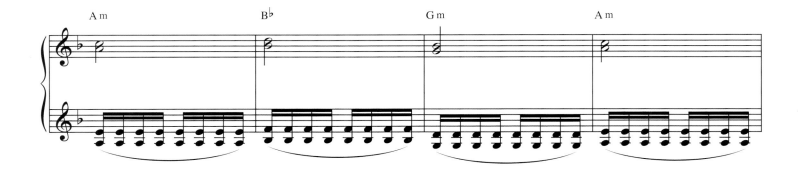

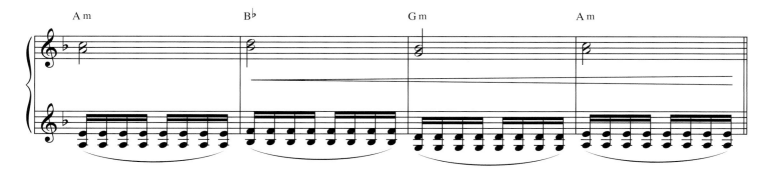

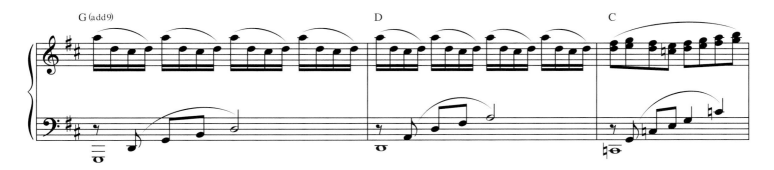

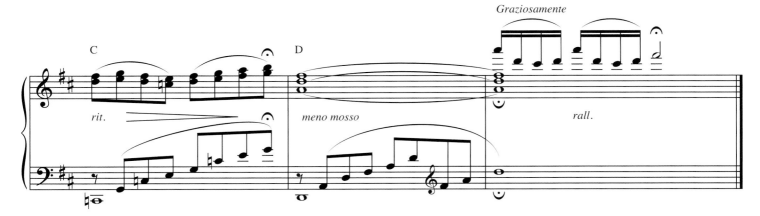

Blue Note

Music by
Emily Bear

Smooth, quasi rubato ♩ = ca. 96

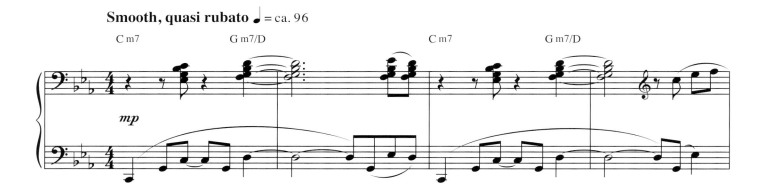

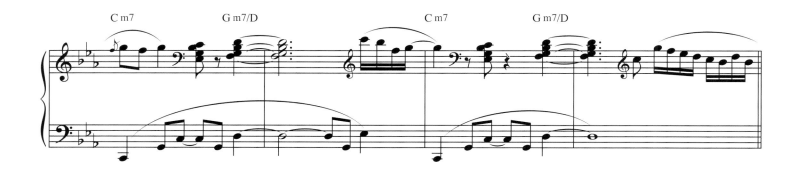

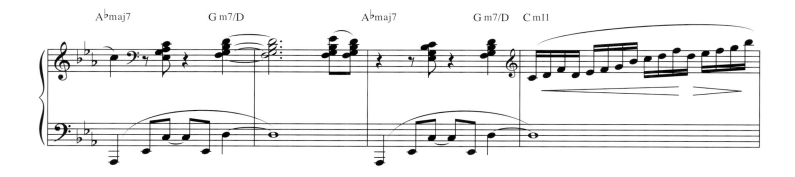

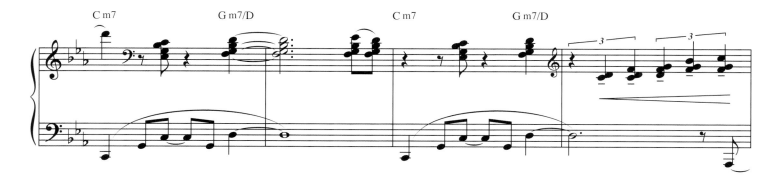

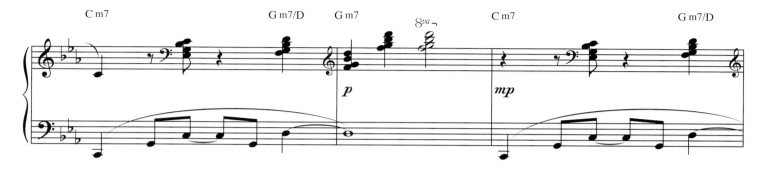

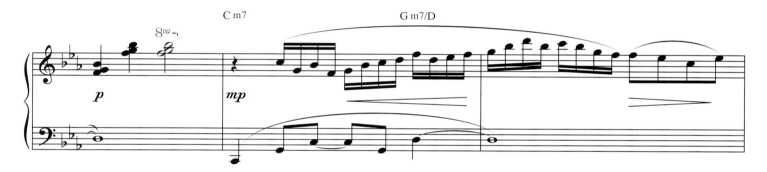

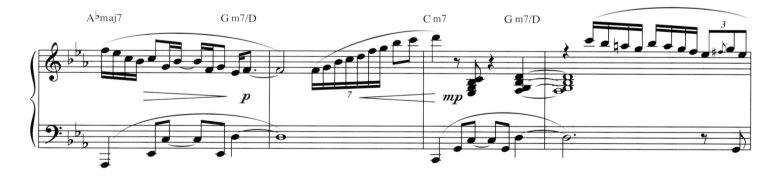

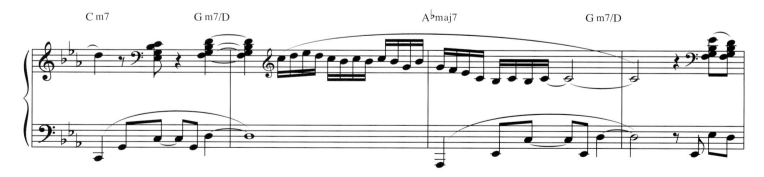

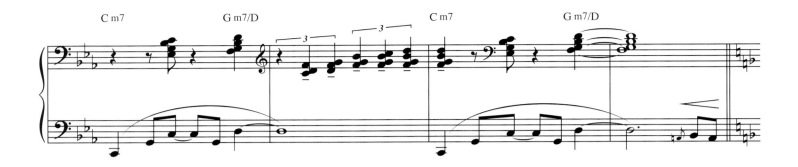

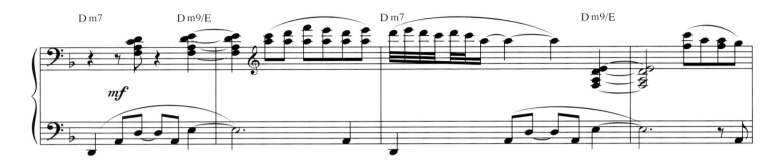

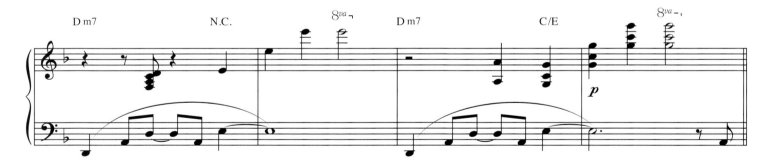

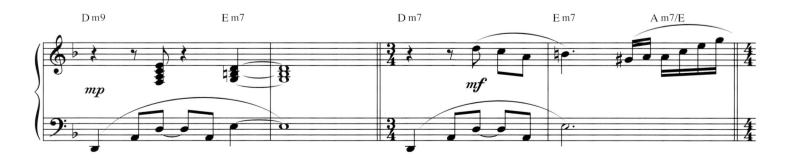

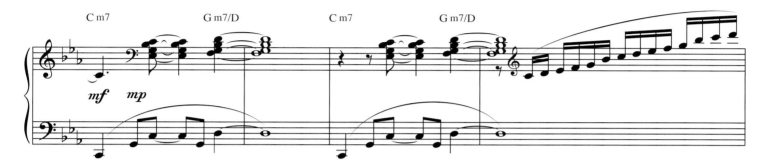

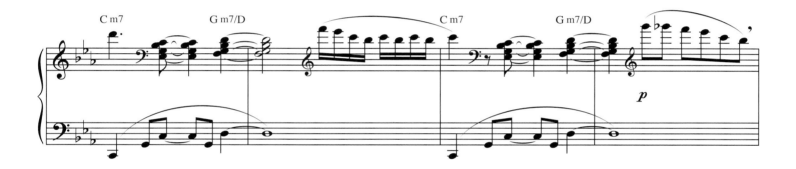

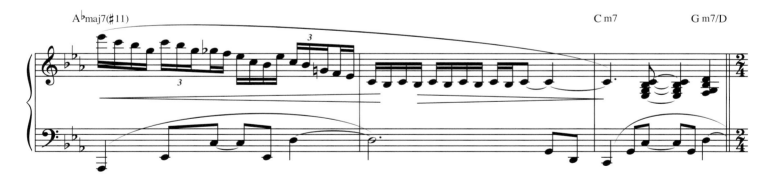

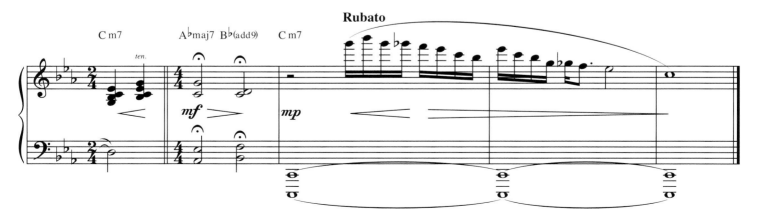

Diversity

Music by
Emily Bear

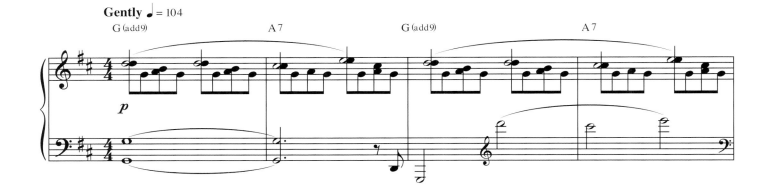

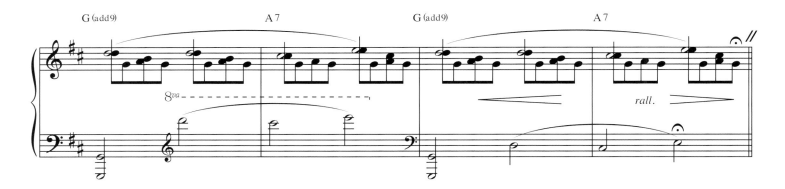

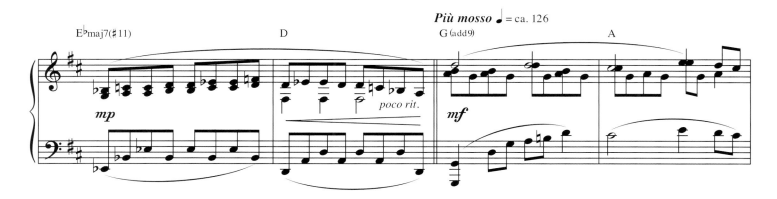

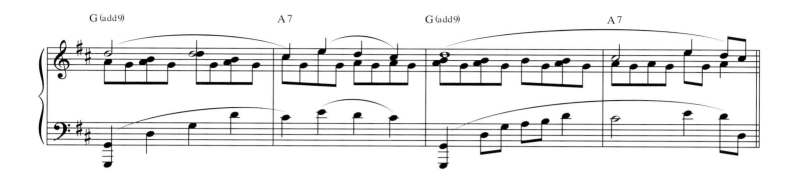

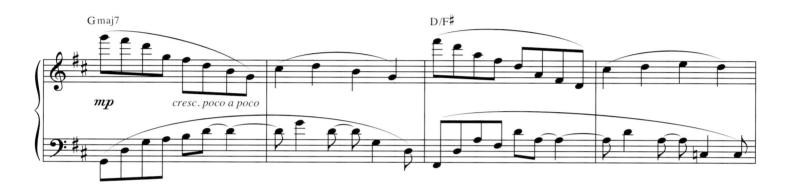

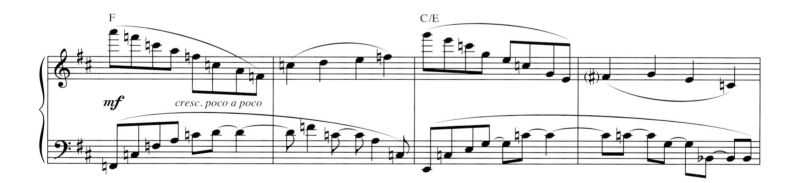

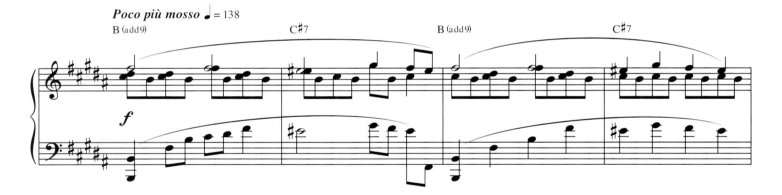

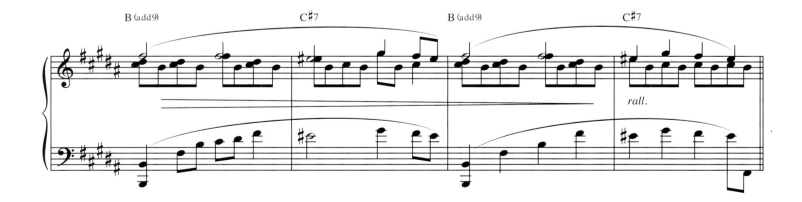

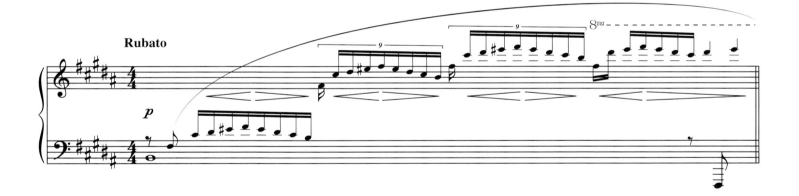

Hot Peppers

Music by
Emily Bear

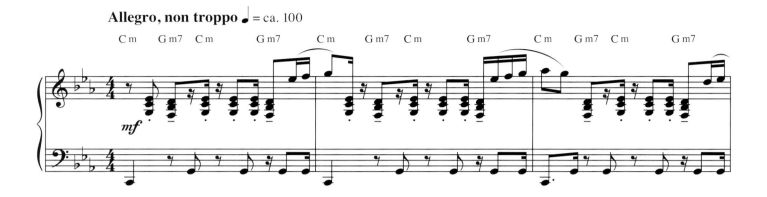

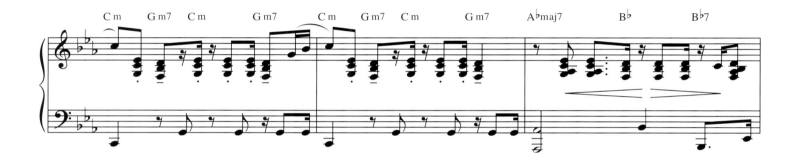

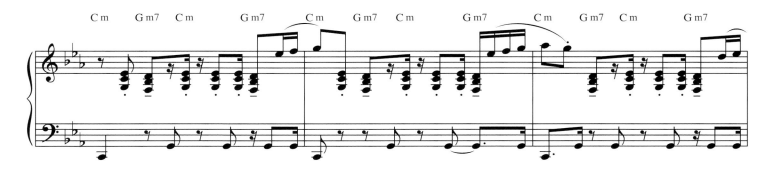

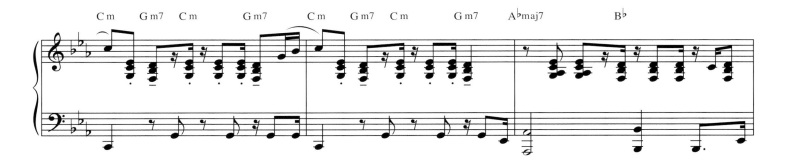

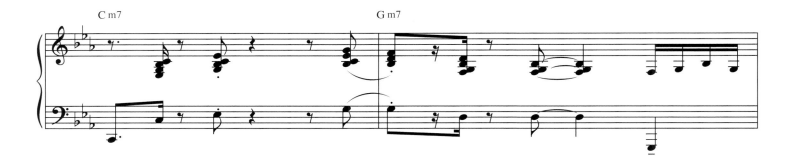

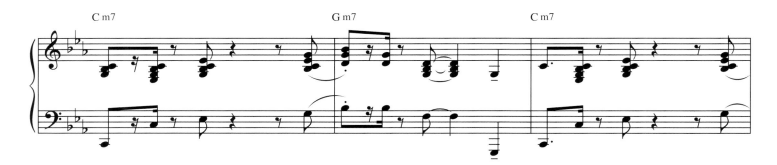

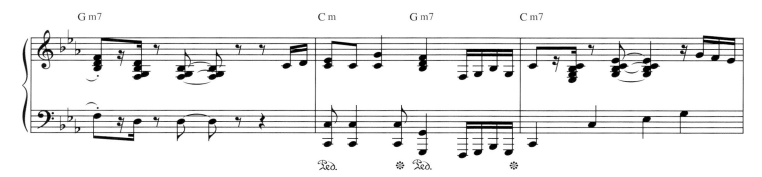

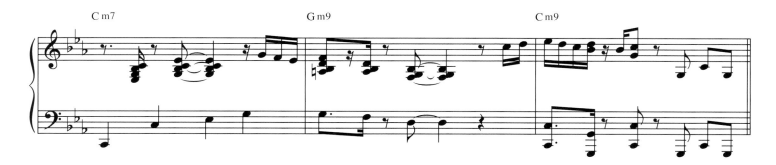

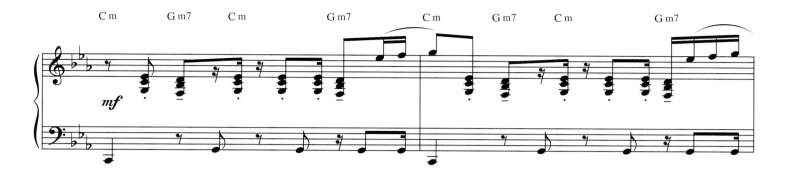

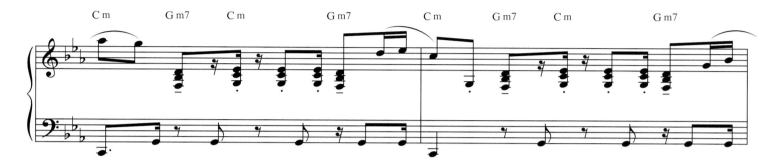

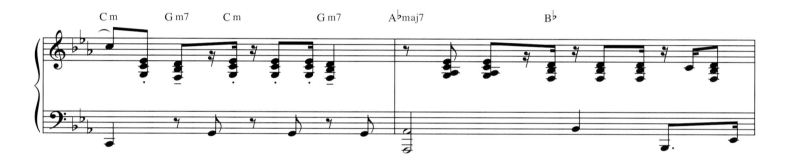

ALIKA

MUSIC BY
EMILY BEAR

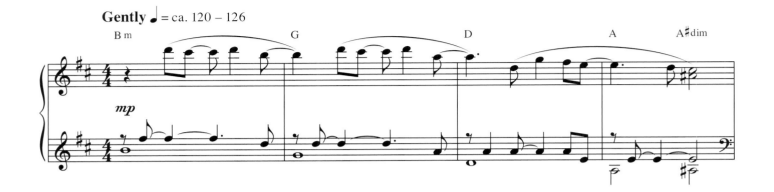

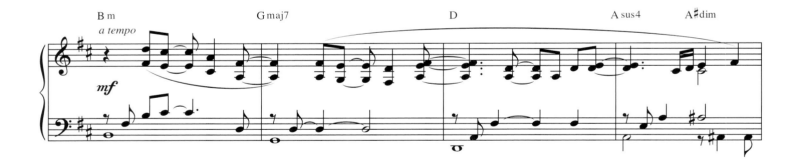

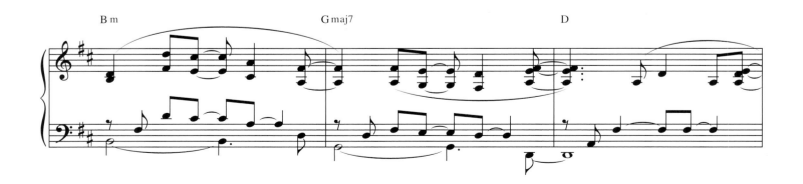

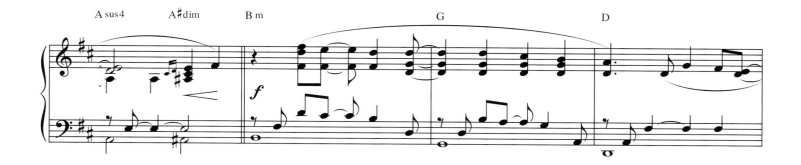

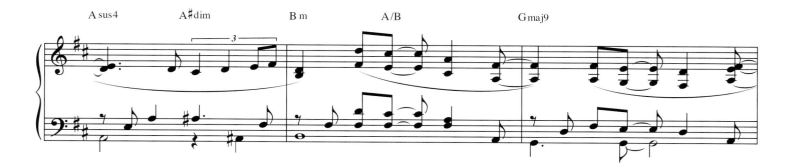

Poco più mosso

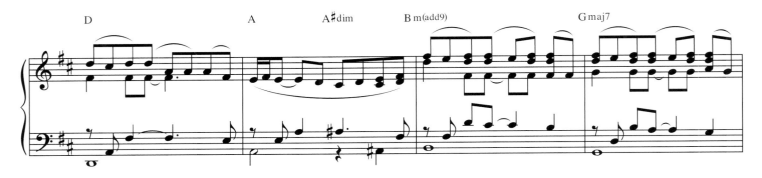

Tempo I

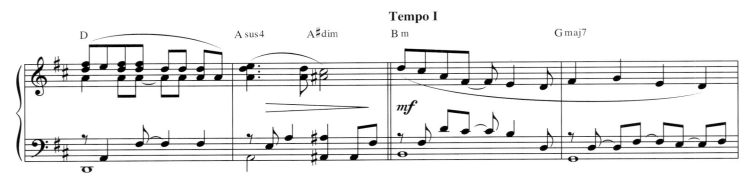

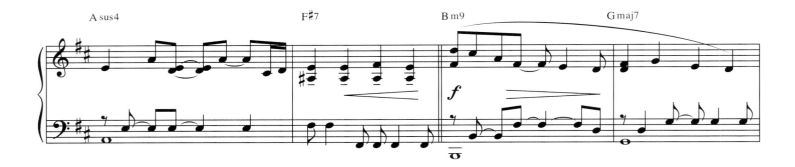

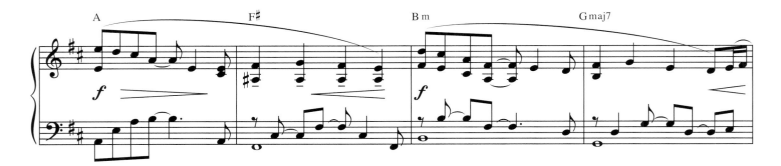

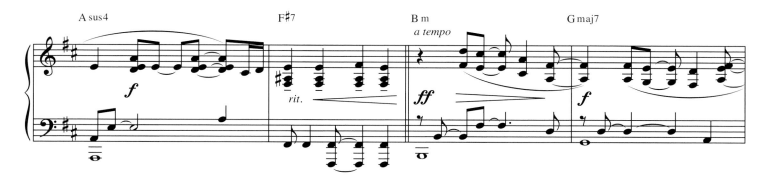

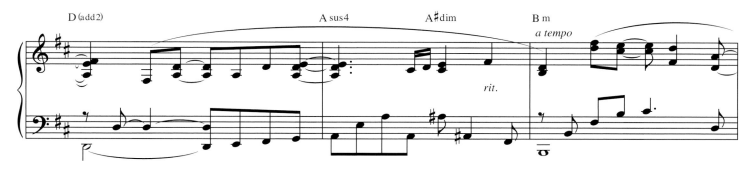

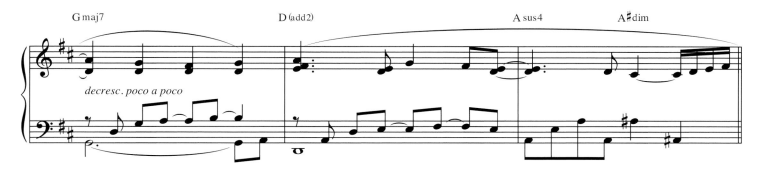

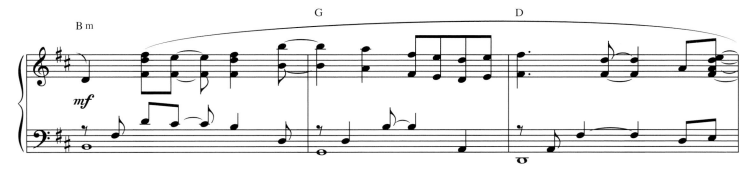

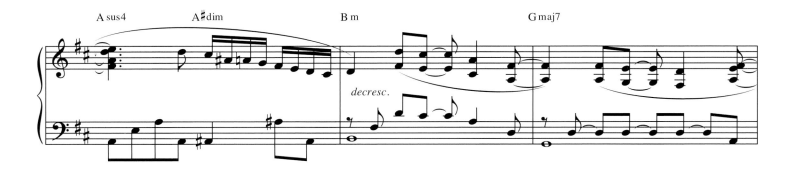

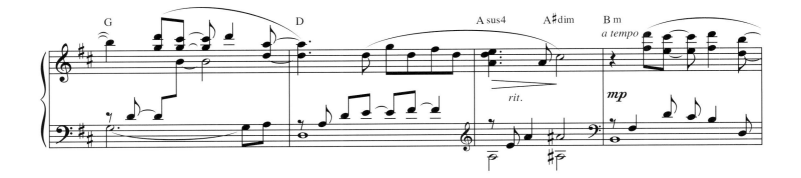

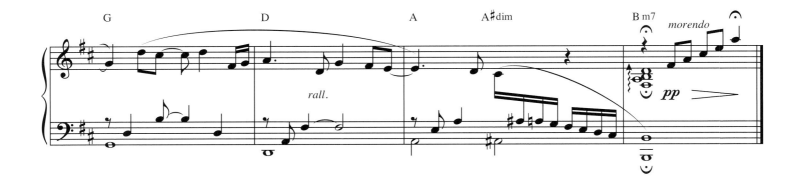

Peralada

MUSIC BY
EMILY BEAR

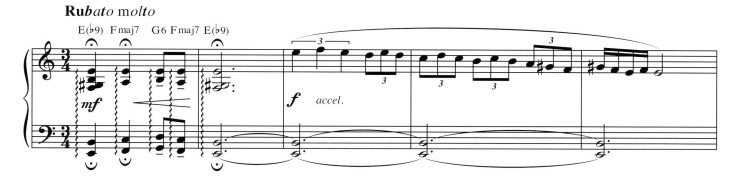

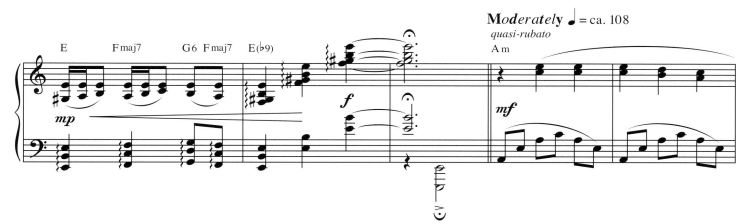

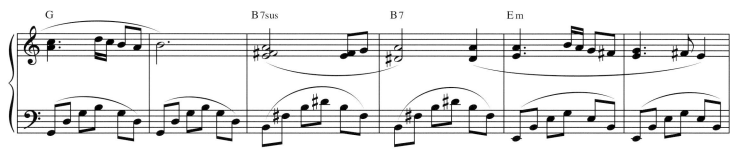

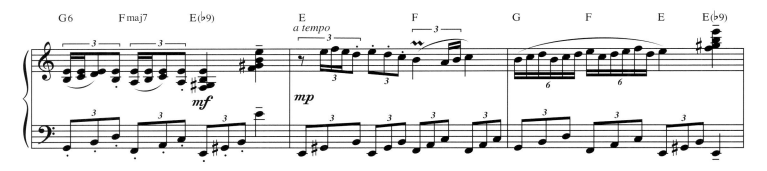

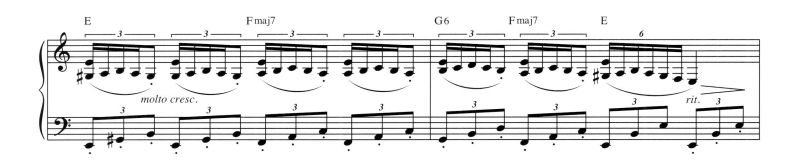

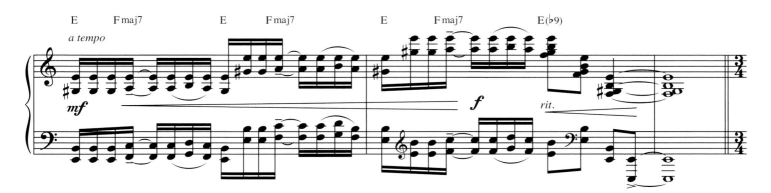

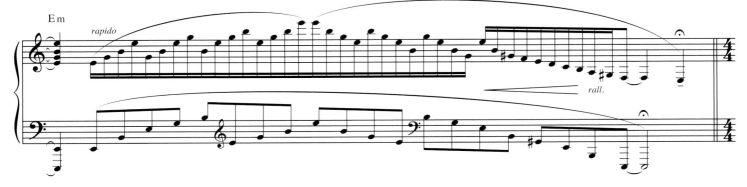

Spiñata

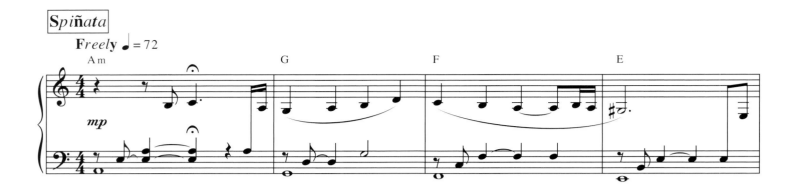

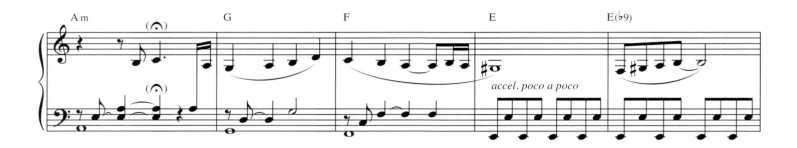

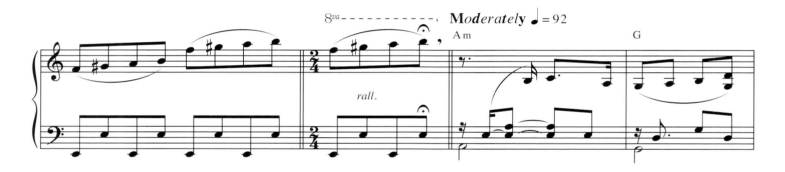

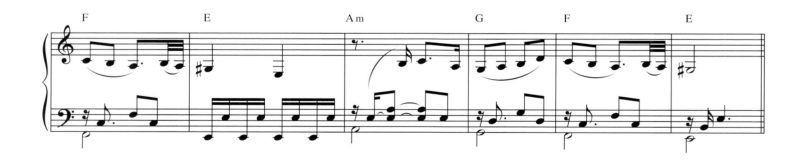

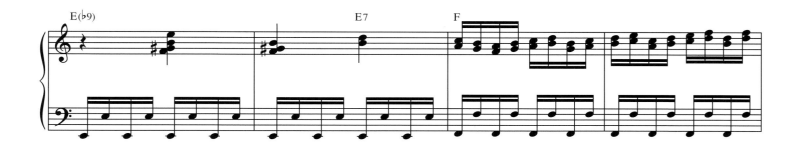

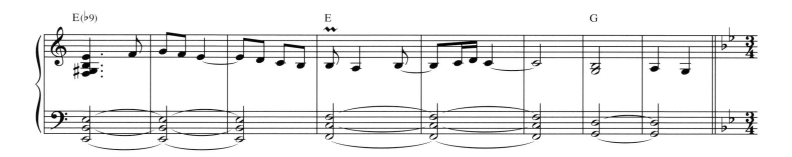

Flam**eng**o

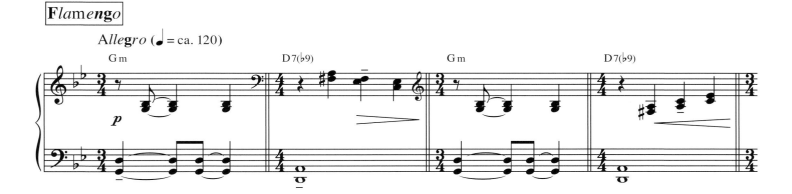

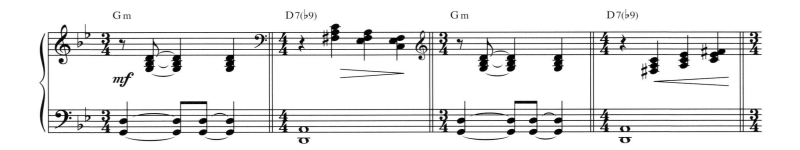

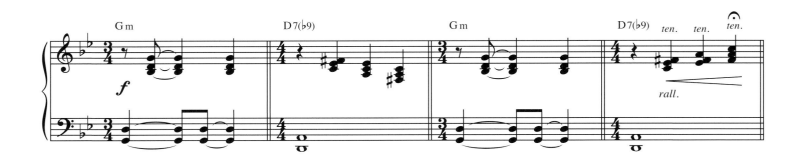

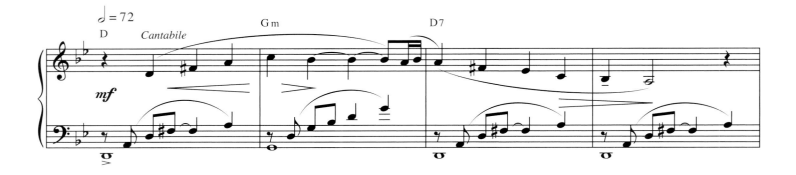

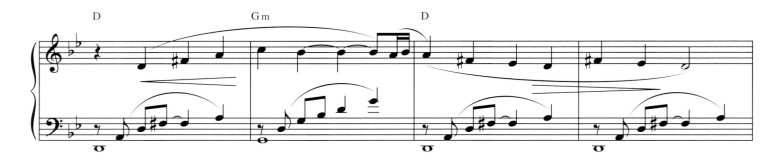

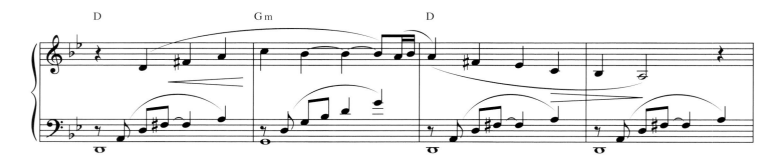

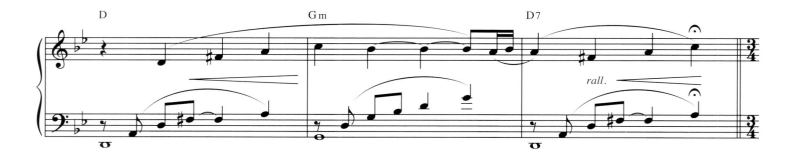

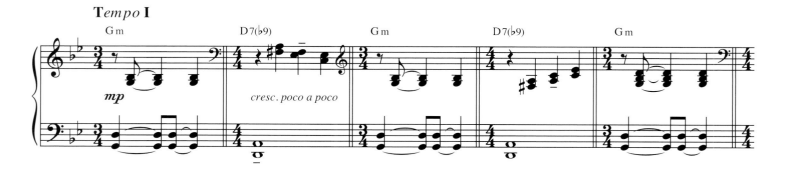

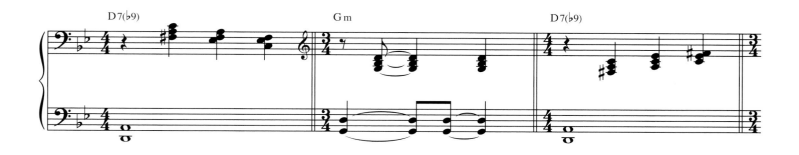

Rubato

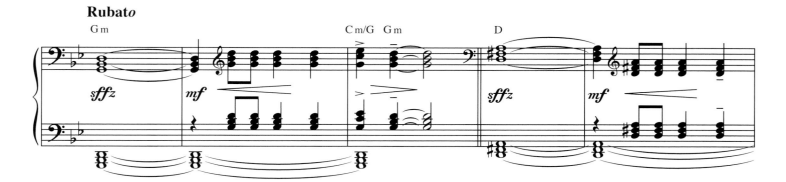

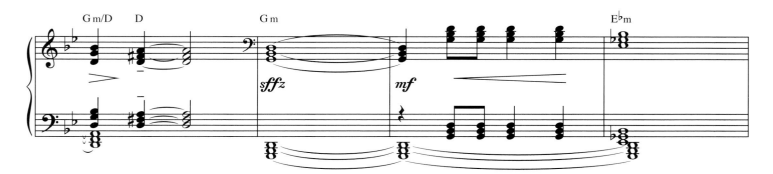

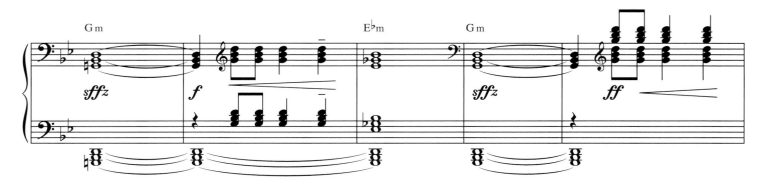

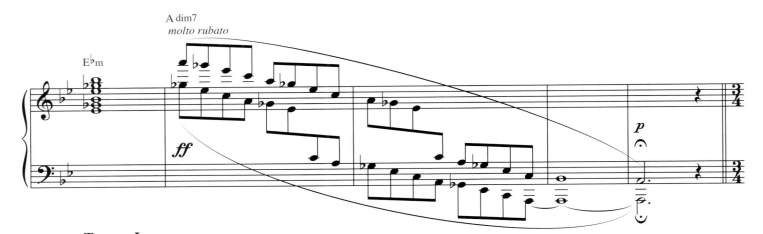

Tempo I

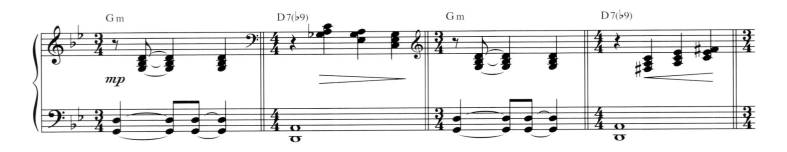

Jessie's Song

Music by
Emily Bear

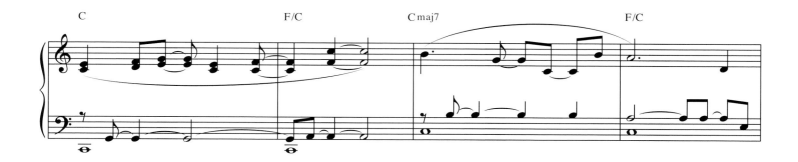

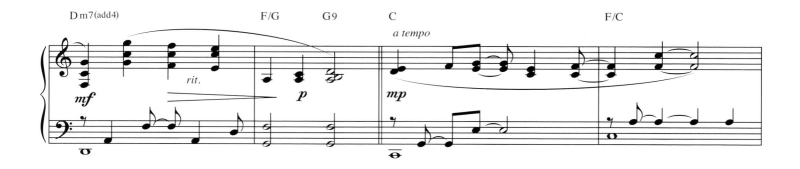

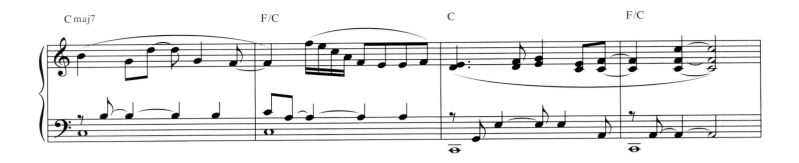

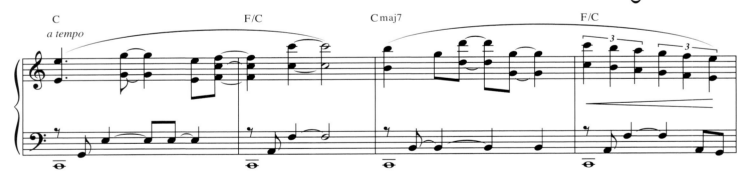

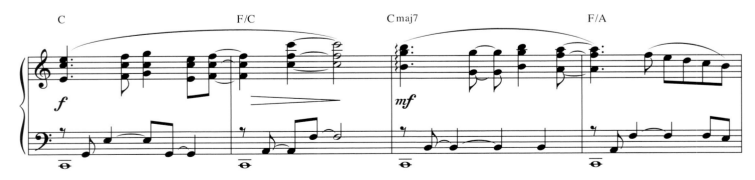

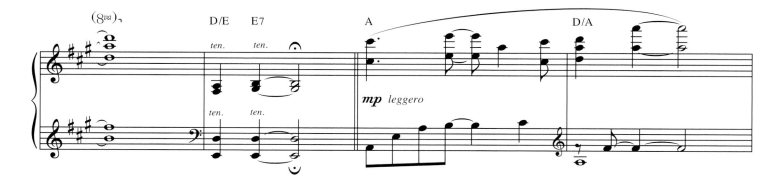

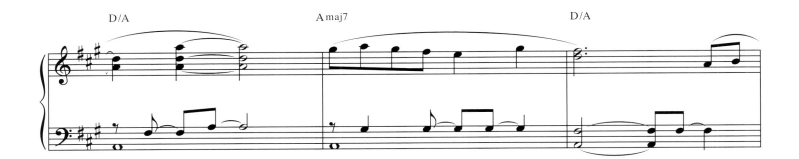

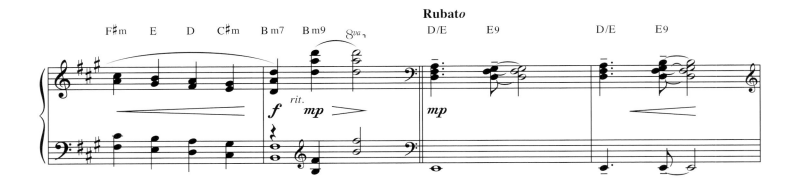

Jazz Angles

Music by
Emily Bear

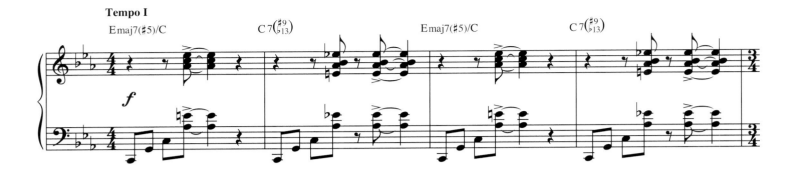

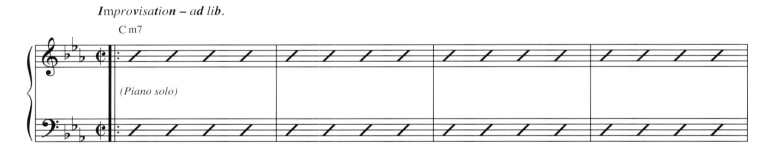

Improvisation – *ad lib*.

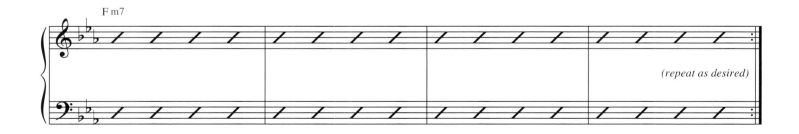

46

C m6

mf *mp*

(*...end piano solo*)

Tempo I

Emaj7(♯5)/C   C 7(♯9♭13)   Emaj7(♯5)/C

ff

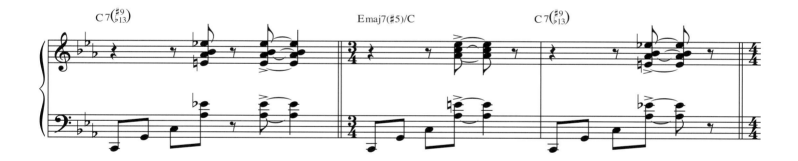

C 7(♯9♭13)   Emaj7(♯5)/C   C 7(♯9♭13)

Emaj7(♯5)/C   *Straight 8ths*   15*ma*

ff   *Glissando*

ITALIA

MUSIC BY
EMILY BEAR

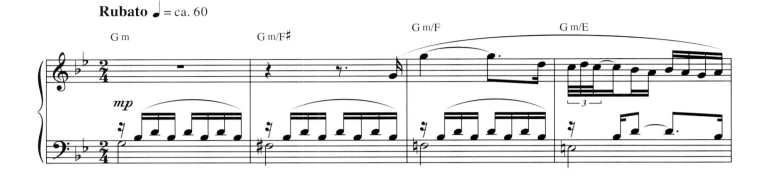

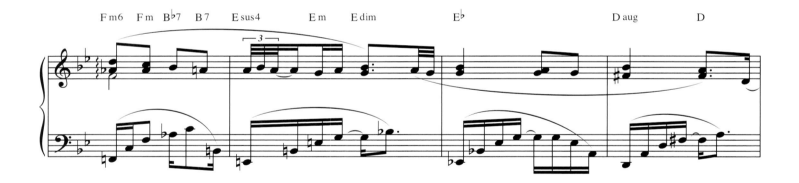

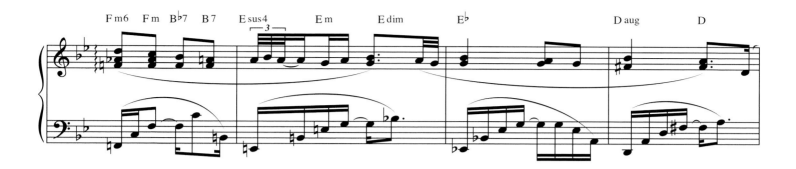

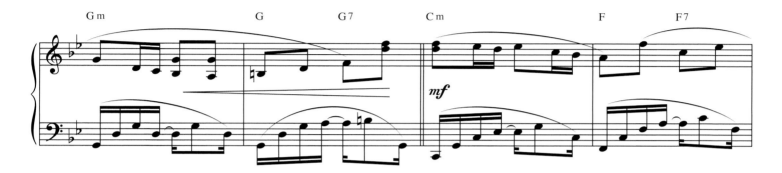

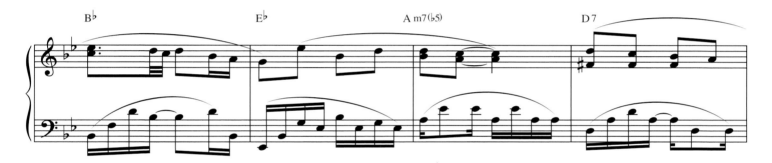

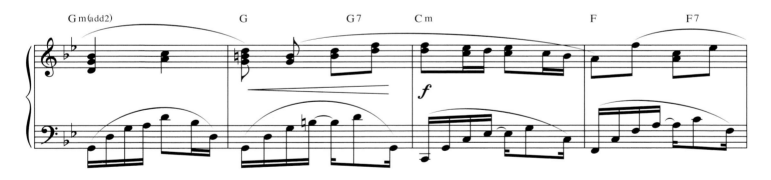

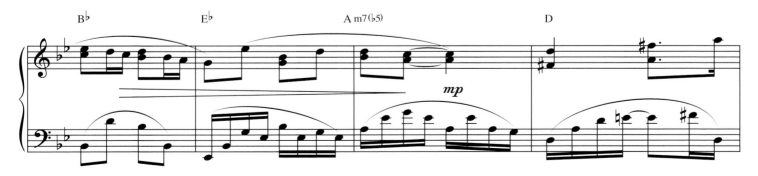

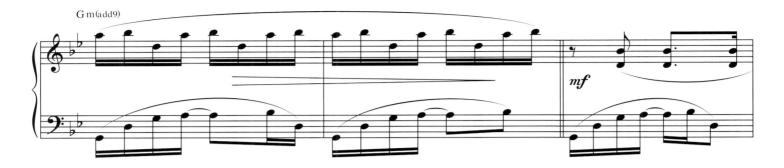

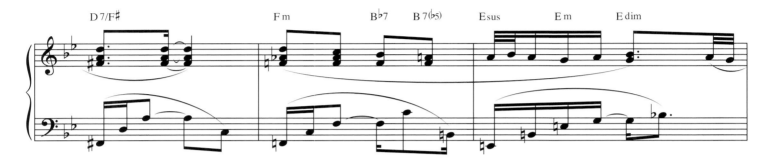

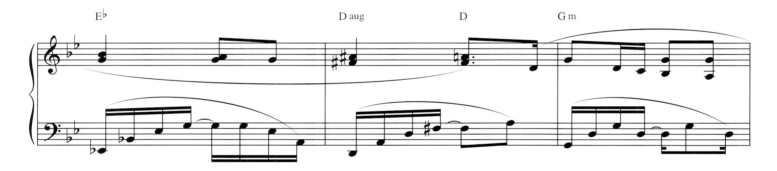

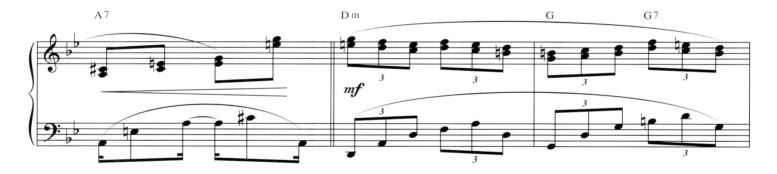

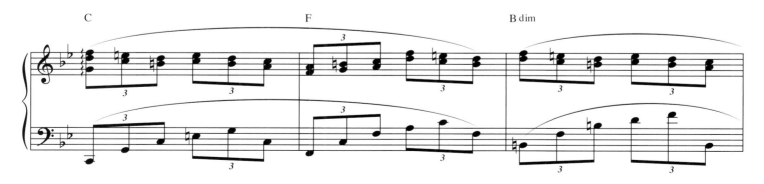

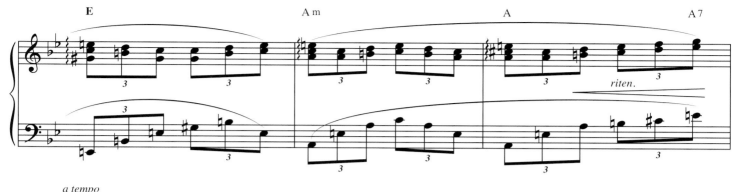

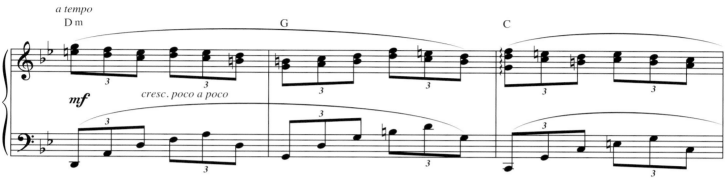

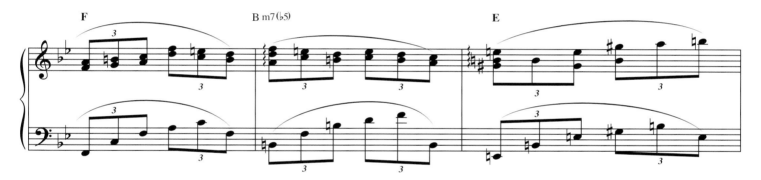

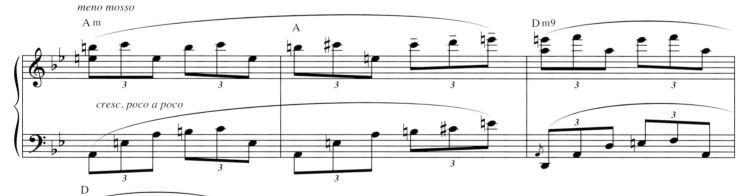

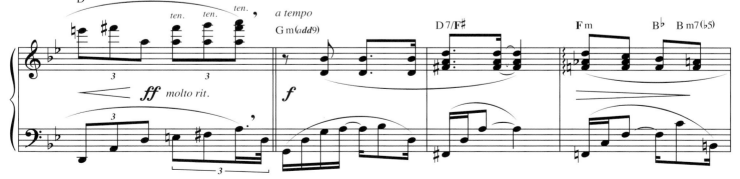

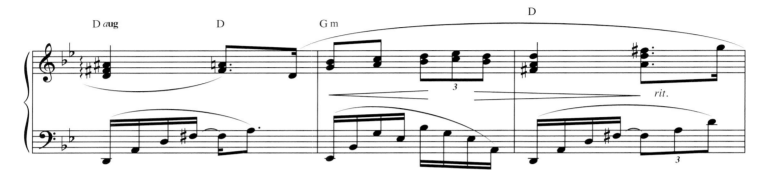

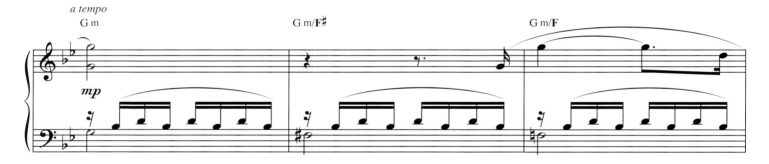

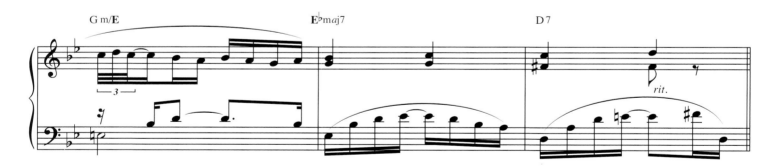

Salsa Americana

MUSIC BY
EMILY BEAR

Moderately ♩ = ca. 88

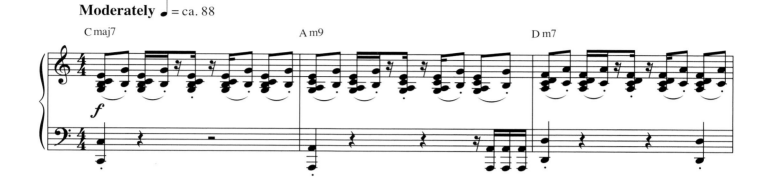

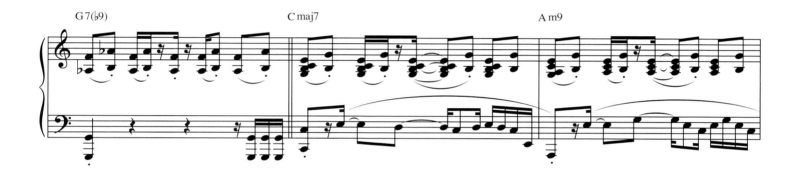

Songs courtesy of Jordan King Music USA (ASCAP).

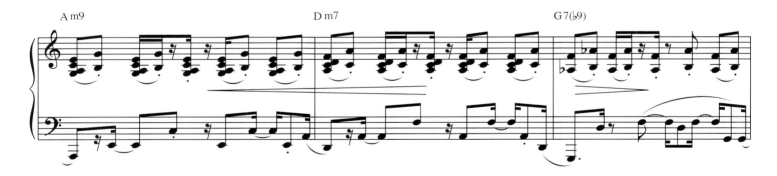

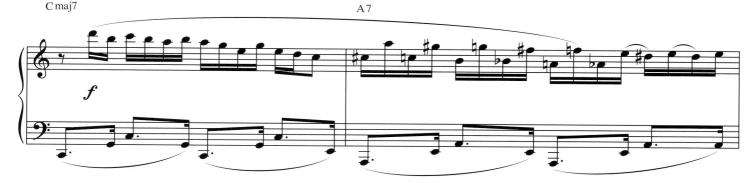

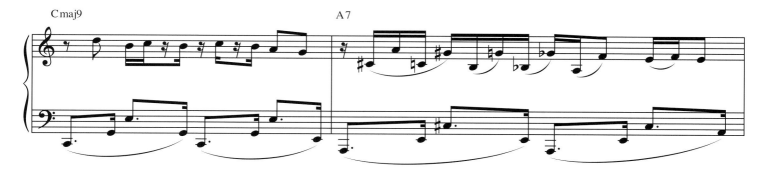

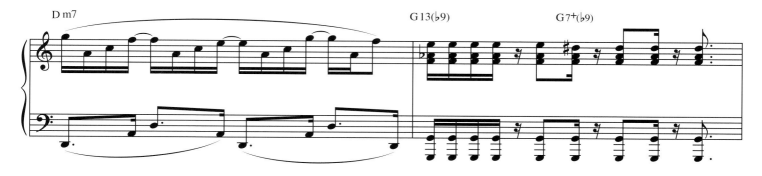

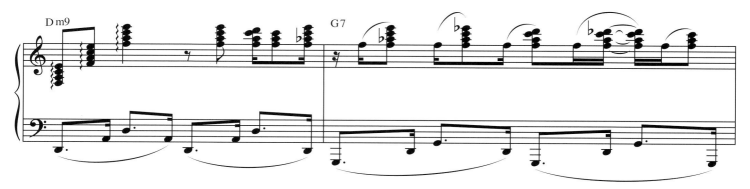

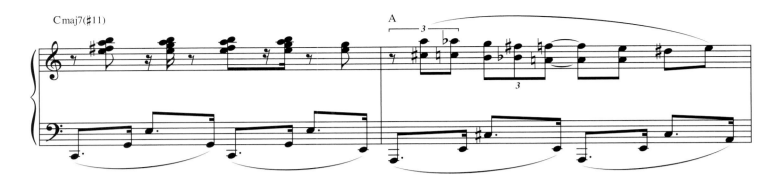

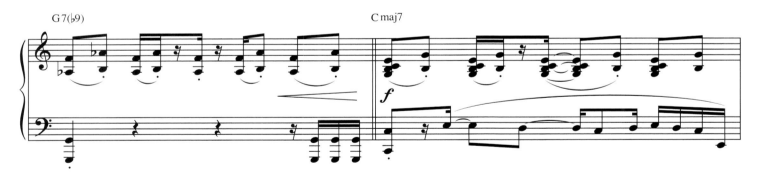

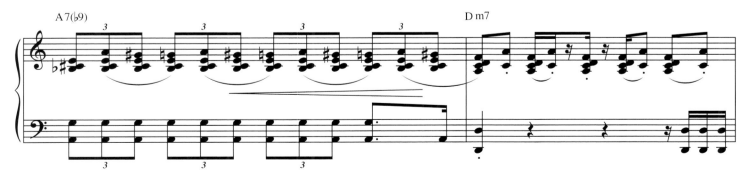

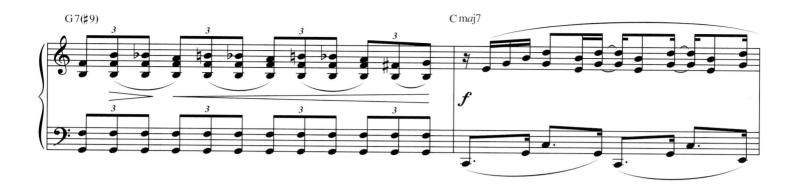

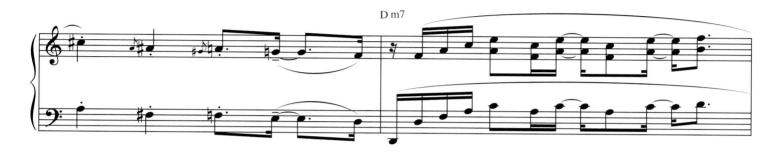

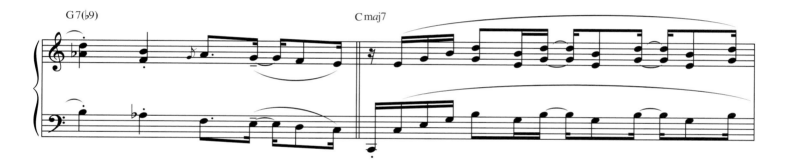

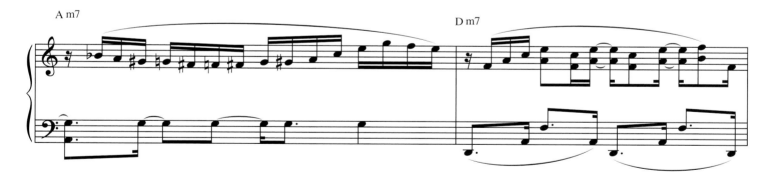

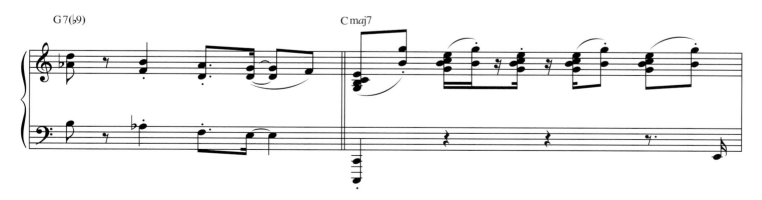

TUTTI CUORE

MUSIC BY
EMILY BEAR

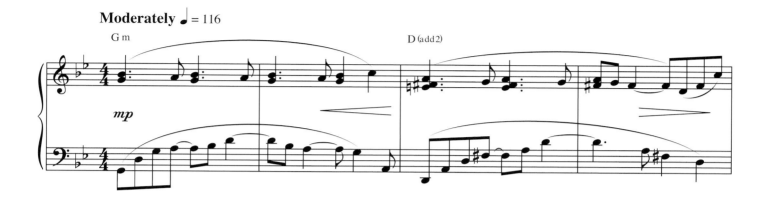

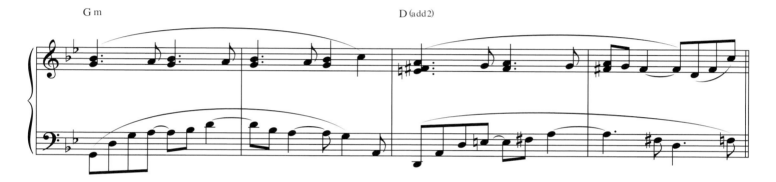

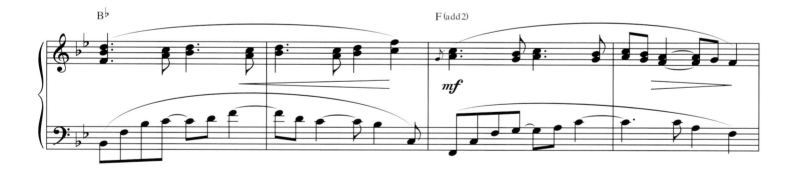

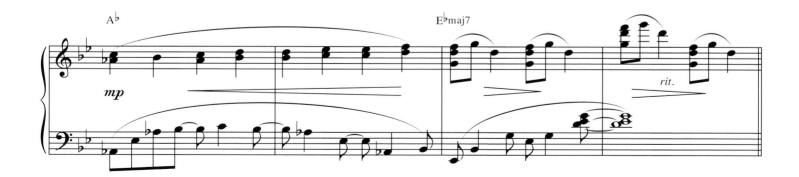

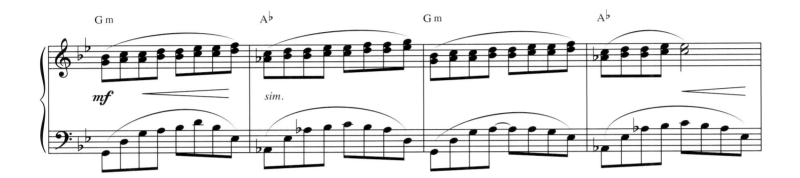

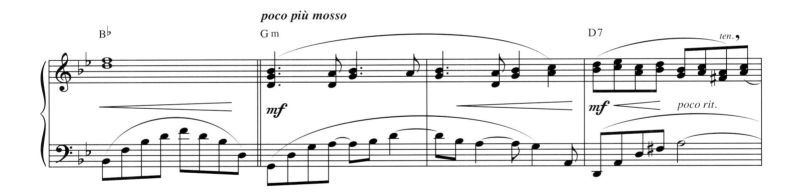

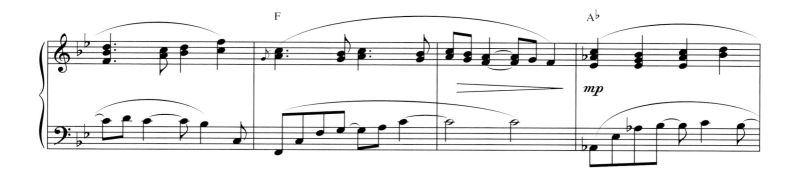

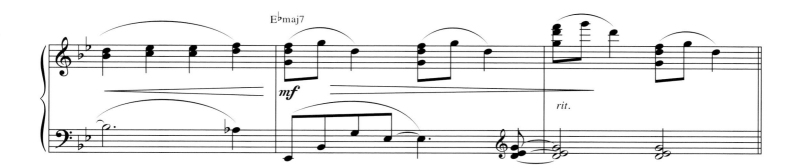

Più mosso
Flowing, quasi rubato

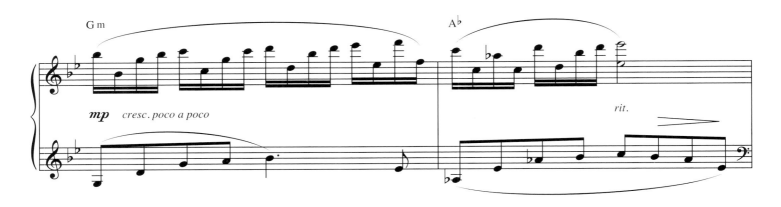

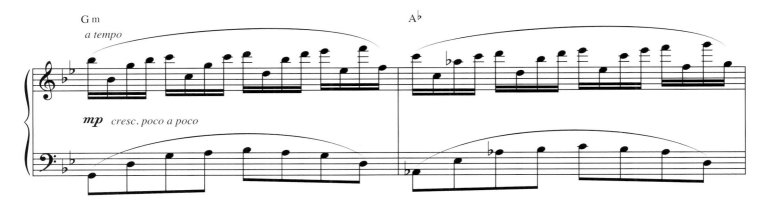

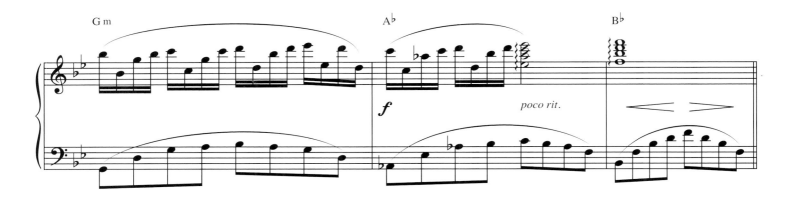

Tempo I

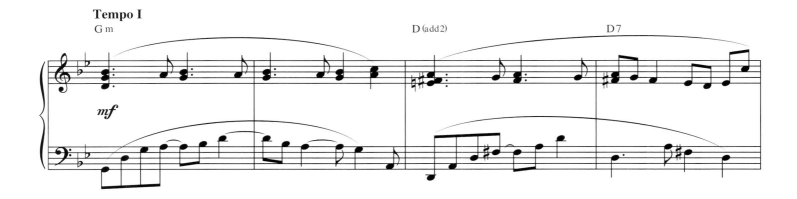

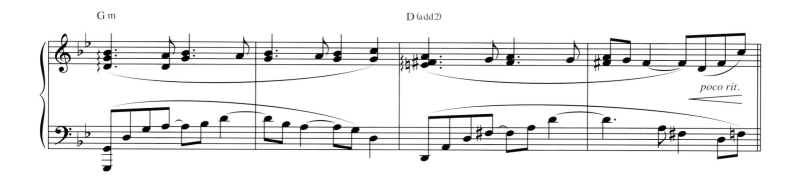

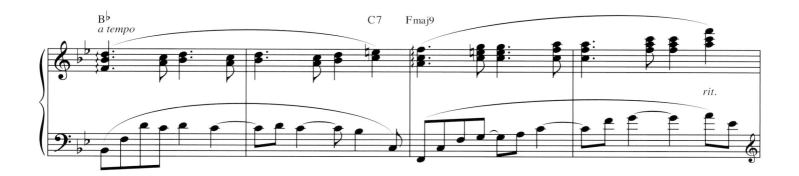

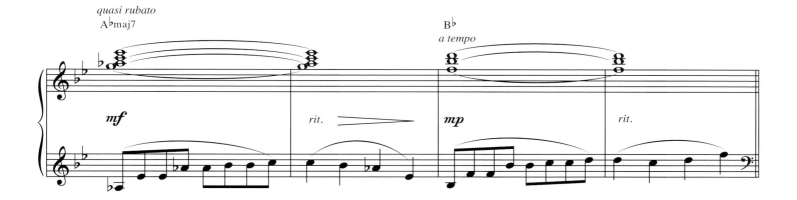

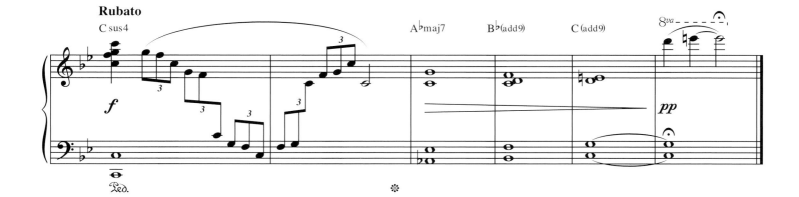

63

Reflections

Music by
Emily Bear

Andante ♩ = ca. 60 – 66

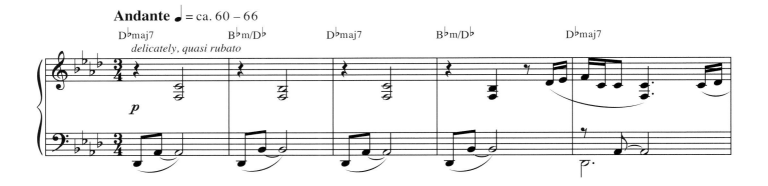

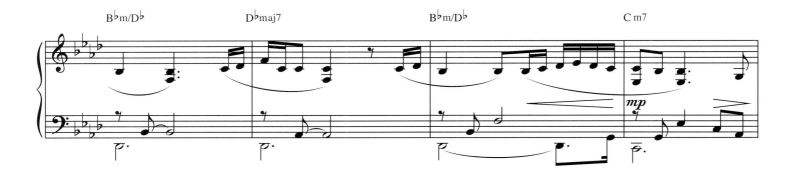

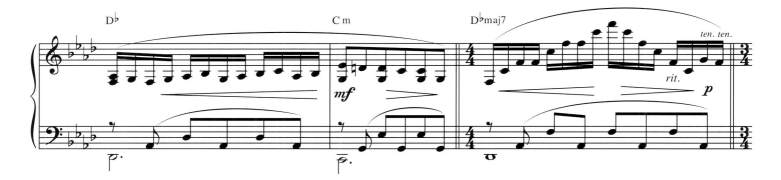

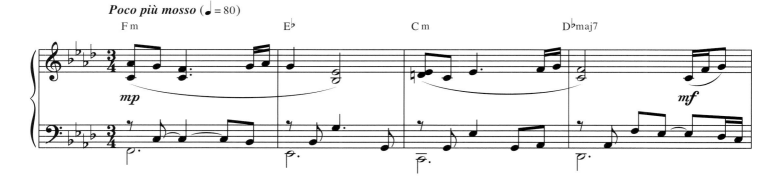

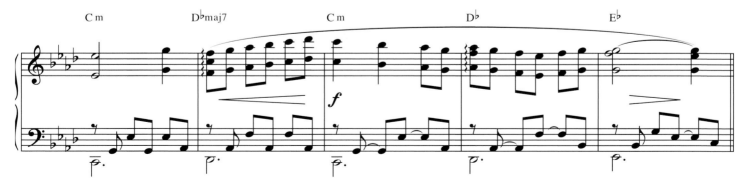

poco più mosso

a tempo

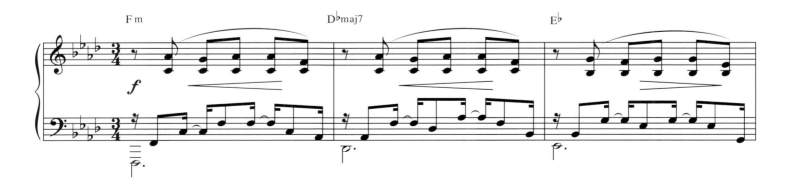

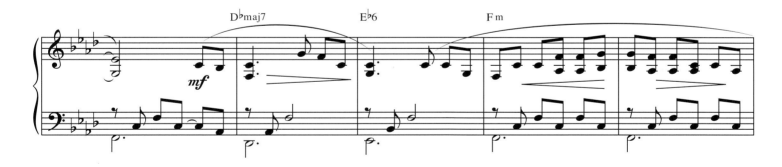

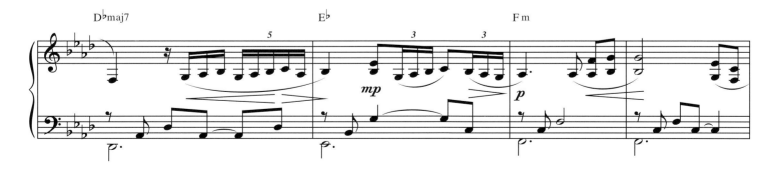

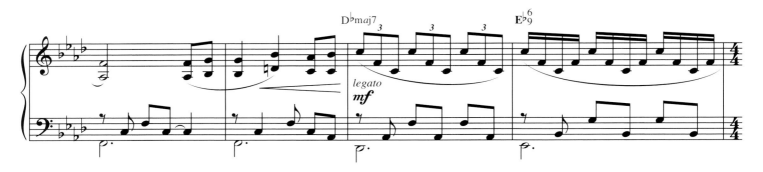

68

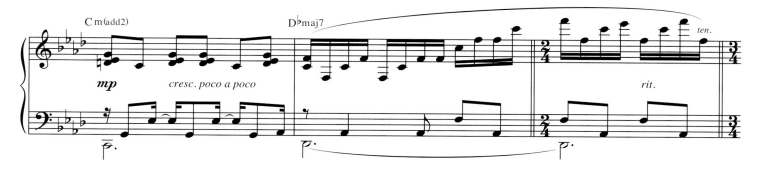

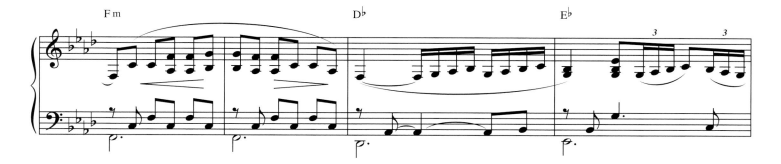

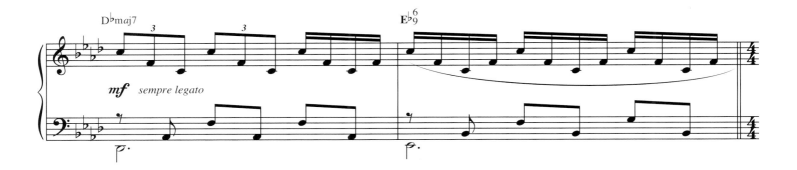

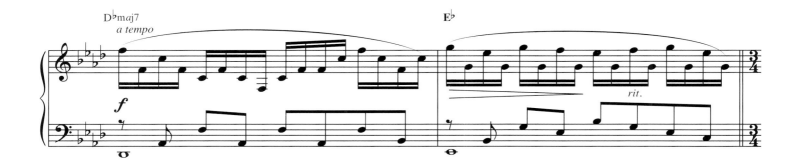

Q

MUSIC BY
EMILY BEAR

Rubato, gently flowing ♩ = ca. 120

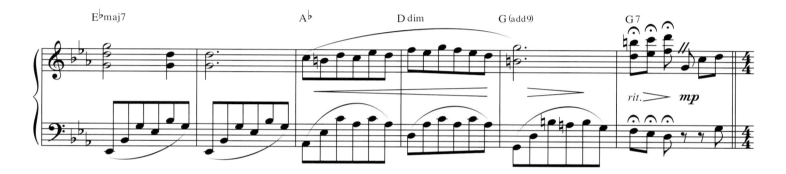

Poco più mosso – quasi rubato

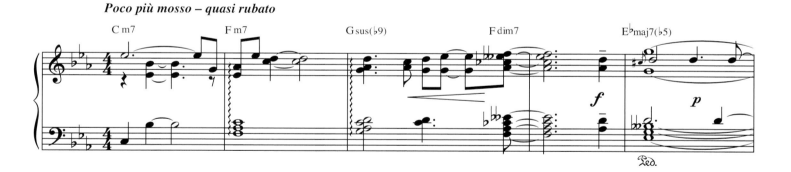

Quickly ♩ = ca. 168 – 176

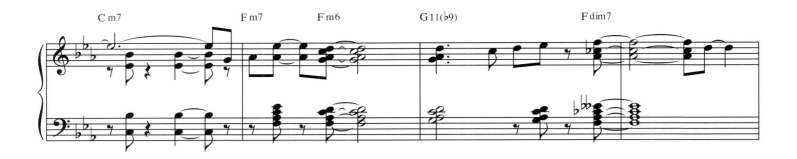

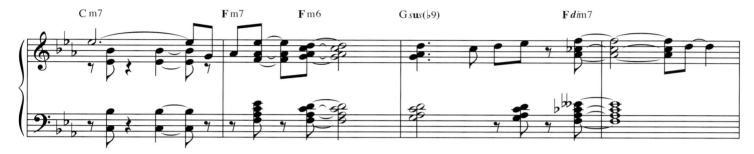

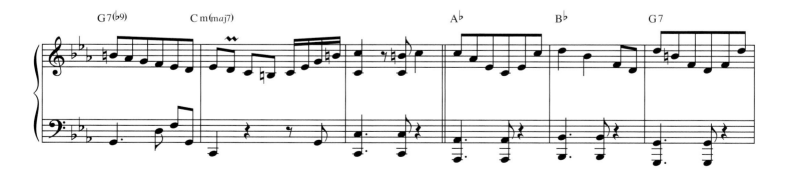

73

Improvisation – ad lib.

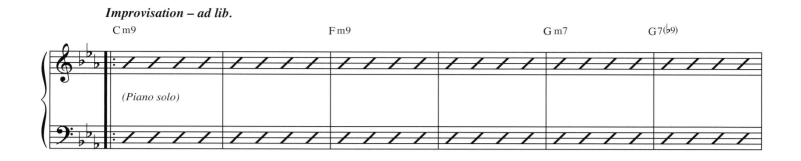

(Piano solo)

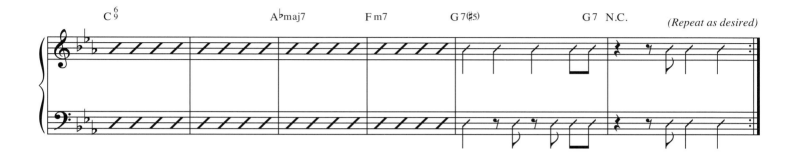

(Repeat as desired)

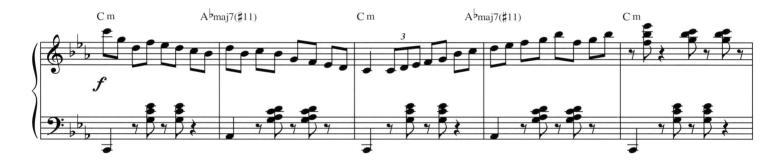

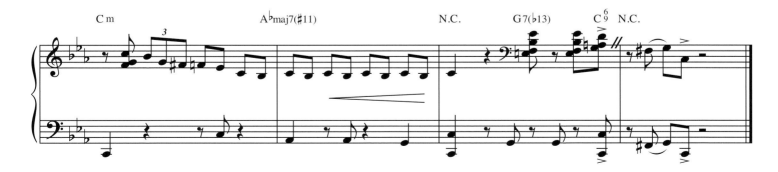

CD Produced by **QUINCY JONES** for

EXECUTIVE PRODUCERS: **QUINCY JONES** AND **JOHN BURK**

CO-EXECUTIVE PRODUCER: **ADAM FELL**

RECORDED BY **SETH PRESANT** AT
WESTLAKE STUDIOS, LOS ANGELES, CA

ZUILL BAILEY RECORDED BY **JOE CUETO, BARRY AN-DERSON,** AND **TED KELLEY** AT
EL ADOBE RECORDING STUDIOS, EL PASO, TX

ASSISTED BY **STEVE RUSCH** AND
BEN SIMONETTI

MIXED BY **SETH PRESANT** AT
THE VILLAGE STUDIOS, LOS ANGELES, CA

MASTERED BY **PAUL BLAKEMORE** AT
CMG MASTERING

PHOTOGRAPHY: **NICK SUTTLE**,
DEVIN DEHAVEN AND **ANDREA BEAR**

ART DIRECTION: **ALBERT J. ROMAN**

EMILY BEAR – PIANO

CARLITOS DEL PUERTO – BASS

FRANCISCO MELA – DRUMS

ZUILL BAILEY – CELLO ("ITALIA," "TUTTI COURE,"
"DIVERSITY," AND "NORTHERN LIGHTS")

ZUILL BAILEY APPEARS COURTESY OF
TELARC INTERNATIONAL

FRANCISCO MELA APPEARS COURTESY OF
HALF NOTE RECORDS

ALL SONGS COMPOSED BY **EMILY BEAR**,
JORDAN KING MUSIC, USA (ASCAP)

WWW.EMILYBEAR.COM

Artist Representation/Management:
QUINCY JONES PRODUCTIONS — **WWW.QUINCYJONES.COM**

For a complete listing of the many recordings available from Concord Music Group, please visit our website at